EXTRATERRESTRIAL LIFE

The Search for Extraterrestrial Life

Stuart A. Kallen

ReferencePoint Press®

San Diego, CA

© 2012 ReferencePoint Press, Inc.
Printed in the United States

For more information, contact:
ReferencePoint Press, Inc.
PO Box 27779
San Diego, CA 92198
www.ReferencePointPress.com

LIBRARY OF CONGRESS CATALOGING-IN-PUBLICATION DATA

Kallen, Stuart A., 1955–
  The search for extraterrestrial life / by Stuart A. Kallen.
    p. cm. — (Extraterrestrial life series)
  Includes bibliographical references and index.
  ISBN-13: 978-1-60152-171-2 (hardback : alk. paper)
  ISBN-10: 1-60152-171-5 (hardback : alk. paper) 1. Life on other planets—Juvenile literature.
  2. Extraterrestrial beings—Juvenile literature. I. Title.
  QB54.K35 2011
  999—dc22
                                         2010052487

CONTENTS

INTRODUCTION

Exploring an Infinite Universe

French scientist Jean d'Alembert once wrote that Jupiter, Saturn, Mars, and Venus all receive light from the sun and are covered with mountains. D'Alembert notes that "it seems to follow that these planets have lakes, have seas; in a word, that they are bodies resembling . . . the earth. Consequently . . . nothing prevents us from believing that the planets are inhabited."[1]

D'Alembert wrote those words in 1765 after studying the planets through a primitive hand-held telescope. While he believed—erroneously as it turns out—that humanlike aliens lived on Jupiter, the idea that the presence of water might signal life on other planets was ahead of his time. Nearly 250 years later, scientists continue to seek out water in their search for extraterrestrial, or ET, life.

Sextillions of Stars

The popular notion of alien life in the twenty-first century has been shaped by books and films. People generally think of extraterrestrials as little green men, robotic humanoids, or monstrous reptiles. However, most scientists who search for alien life in Earth's solar system do not expect to find sentient beings, that is, conscious creatures who possess intelligence. Instead they study planetary environments that might sustain single-cell or multicell life. For example, space probes to the moon, Mars, Jupiter, and Saturn have searched for traces of water, oxygen, and other physical elements that might be favorable to microscopic life.

Planetary scientists have yet to discover any life in the solar system, but some believe that intelligent beings do exist elsewhere in the universe. Astronomers estimate the universe contains 70 sextillion stars that are similar in temperature or size to the sun. Based on calculations by astrophysicists Charles Lineweaver and Daniel Grether at the University of New South Wales, Australia, at least 25 percent of those stars have planets, called exoplanets, or planets outside of Earth's solar system. If the figures are accurate, trillions of exoplanets exist in the countless galaxies of the universe. According to Lineweaver, "the rapidity with which life arose on Earth suggests that more than 10 percent of [the trillions of] planets have life."[2] While Lineweaver believes most of the life is microscopic bacteria, the sheer number of living environments indicates sentient beings might exist beyond Earth's solar system.

> **DID YOU KNOW?**
>
> Seventy sextillion, which is the estimated number of sun-like stars in the universe, is equal to 7,000 trillion, or the number 70 followed by 21 zeros.

Trillions of Miles from Earth

Scientists searching for intelligent life on exoplanets are limited by the vast distances of the universe. Aside from the sun, the closest star system to Earth is called Alpha Centauri. It is located over 4.37 light-years, or about 25.7 trillion miles (41.5 trillion km), from Earth. Since traveling a single light-year would take the average spacecraft over 21,000 years, humans are not likely to visit the Alpha Centauri star system in the near future.

While spacecraft are relatively slow, radio waves generated by radio, television, cell phone, and other signals from Earth, travel as fast as light.

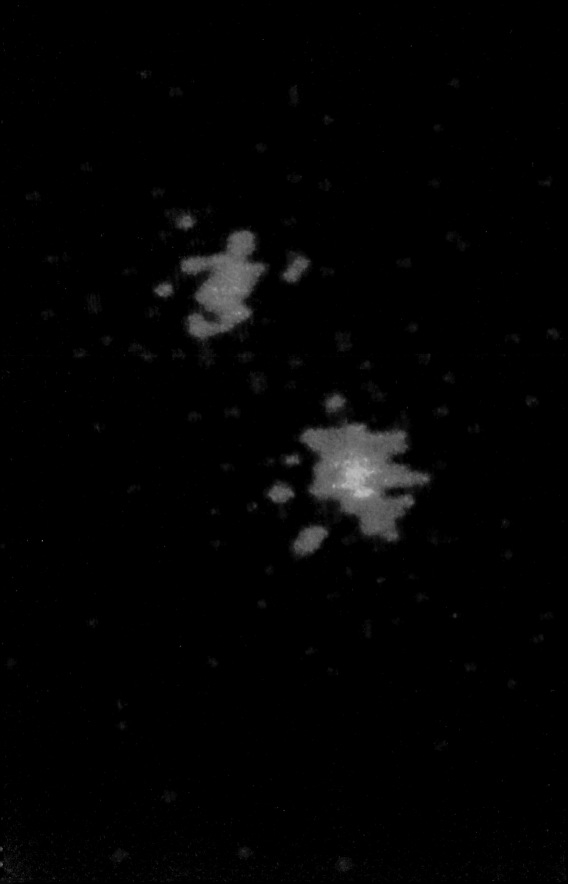

The search for extraterrestrial life is complicated by the vast distances between star systems. It would take many thousands of years to reach the nearest star system to Earth, Alpha Centauri. A colored X-ray image shows two of the brightest stars in the Alpha Centauri system.

Some scientists believe that advanced civilizations on other planets might be generating radio waves just as humans have done on Earth. These scientists have searched the skies for alien radio waves since 1960 when astronomer Frank Drake pointed a radio telescope at the stars to listen for chatter. So far, the only radio waves detected in the universe have emanated from Earth.

For thousands of years, humans have wondered if they are alone in the vast regions of outer space. While millions of people believe extraterrestrials have visited Earth in spaceships, no one has ever taken a photograph, video, or voice recording of such a being. But this has not stopped planetary scientists from utilizing the most advanced high-tech equipment ever devised to seek out signs of extraterrestrial life.

> **DID YOU KNOW?**
>
> Light travels at a speed of 186,282 miles (300,000km) per second. A light-year is the distance light can travel in a year, equal to about 5.8 trillion miles (9.5 trillion km).

CHAPTER ONE

Looking for Life on the Moon and Mars

On August 25, 1835, the headline in the *New York Sun* announced "Great Astronomical Discoveries Lately Made."[3] The story informed readers that the famous British astronomer Sir John Herschel had made fantastic discoveries about the moon while peering through a new, incredibly powerful telescope located in South Africa. The story went on to say that bison-like creatures, birds, lunar fish, and bearded goatlike animals possessing a single unicorn horn lived on the moon. But these were not the moon's only inhabitants. The moon was also home to intelligent beings described as bipedal beavers. Besides walking on two feet, the newspaper wrote, this creature "carries its young in its arms like a human being. . . . Its huts are constructed better and higher than those of many tribes of human savages, and from the appearance of smoke in nearly all of them, there is no doubt of its being acquainted with the use of fire."[4]

The *Sun* went on to describe lunar humanoids four feet (1.2m) in height covered with glossy, copper-colored hair. Their yellow hairless faces resembled those of orangutans. Several features distinguished these moon people from the earthbound apes, however. They had wings and moved their hands and arms passionately while communicating. The paper noted the aliens appeared innocent and happy. The reporter, R.A. Locke, named the extraterrestrials "man-bats."

The story about the lunar discoveries riveted the attention of New Yorkers, and the *Sun* sold 19,000 copies, making it the best-selling paper in the world that day. No scientist or reporter came forward to dispute the story. Half a dozen other papers, including the respected *New York Times*, wrote their own articles about the lunar man-bats. By early September, however, the story was shown to be a prank. Locke admitted he wrote about the moon creatures to prove how easily the public could be fooled by stories of space aliens.

Waterways on Mars

Locke's story came to be known as the Great Lunar Hoax, but throughout the rest of the nineteenth century, astronomers continued to search the night skies for alien life. By the middle of the century, increasingly

An 1835 news story reported that British astronomer Sir John Herschel had discovered an array of remarkable creatures on the moon, including winged humanoids (dubbed "man-bats") and various animals resembling bison, birds, fish, and goats (all pictured in this 1835 lithograph). The story turned out to be a hoax.

powerful telescopes had found no beavers, bison, man-bats, or other aliens living on the moon, so astronomers turned their attention elsewhere. One of those scientists, Percival Lowell, was from a very wealthy Boston family and spent a considerable amount of his fortune studying Mars.

In 1895 Lowell constructed an observatory on a mountain outside the tiny settlement of Flagstaff, Arizona. The Lowell Observatory was the first of its kind, built in a rural area on an elevated site with an altitude of 7,000 feet (2,100m). Lowell built the observatory after studying the work of Giovanni Schiaparelli, a respected Italian astronomer. Schiaparelli wrote about an extensive system of ditches on the Martian surface he called *canali*. The Italian word *canali* translates into English as either "channels" or "canals"; however, these words have different meanings.

Channels are gullies, or small valleys, created by natural forces such as wind and water. Canals are artificial waterways for navigation, irrigation, or drainage.

Between 1877 and 1890 Schiaparelli published a series of maps of the Martian *canali* as he observed them through his telescope. If he was aware of the difference between the English words "channels" and "canals" he made no mention of it. Whatever the case, the idea that intelligent beings built canals on Mars caught on with the public and generated great debate among scientists.

Lowell was convinced that the canals had been built by sentient beings. After opening his observatory, Lowell spent night after night peering at Mars through the facility's 12-inch telescope (30.4cm), an instrument similar to those used by today's amateur astronomers.

Lowell wrote about his observations in the 1895 book *Mars*. He said he counted 184 canals on the planet, more than double the number recorded by Schiaparelli. Lowell theorized that the canals were filled with

The Canals of Mars

In 1892 Giovanni Schiaparelli published an article with a map of Martian canals in the British journal *Science* with the following comments:

> The lines of [the canals] run from one to another of the dark spots of Mars usually called seas, and form a very well-marked network over the bright part of the surface. Their arrangement seems constant and permanent (at least so far as can be judged by the observations of four and one-half years); but their appearance and the degree of their visibility is not always the same. . . . Sometimes these lines or canals show themselves under the form of diffused and indistinct shading; at other times they appear as very definite and precise markings of uniform tone, as if they had been drawn with a pen. . . . Each canal terminates at its two extremes either in a sea or in another canal.

Quoted in David Hatcher Childress, *Extraordinary Archaeology.* Kempton, IL: Adventures Unlimited, 1999, pp. 171–72.

water that had melted from the Martian polar ice caps. The dark regions seen on Mars, which give it its reddish appearance, were believed to be trees and other vegetation.

Intelligent Water-Dwelling Creatures

Lowell suggested—correctly—that the atmosphere on Mars was too thin to sustain creatures that breathed oxygen. Earth's atmosphere consists of gases such as nitrogen, oxygen, and carbon dioxide (CO_2). The atmosphere protects all life on Earth by absorbing the sun's ultraviolet solar radiation and by keeping temperatures at levels hospitable to life. While Lowell believed the Martian atmosphere could not support life, he thought that the water in the canals teemed with intelligent fishlike creatures. As Lowell wrote, "there is nothing in the world or beyond it to prevent . . . a being with gills . . . from being a most superior person."[5]

Lowell published another book, *Mars and Its Canals*, in 1906, and by this time millions of people were convinced of the existence of Martians. However, in 1907 respected British biologist Alfred Russel Wallace responded to *Mars and Its Canals* with his own book *Is Mars Habitable?* Wallace pointed out that the atmosphere of Mars was so thin that water could not exist there because it would evaporate immediately. Two years later, Greek astronomer Eugène Antoniadi observed Mars though a 32.6-inch telescope (83cm), which was much more powerful than Lowell's optical instrument. Antoniadi clearly saw that Mars had no canals. He said they were an optical illusion most likely created by shadows and light. Lowell died in 1915, still believing that intelligent beings inhabited Mars.

Mariner to Mars

While most scientists accepted the view that flowing water did not exist in canals on Mars, the planet remained a source of fascination for decades. In the 1950s credible astronomers continued to believe that Mars might be home to some sort of alien plant life if not sentient beings. Even into the 1960s, textbooks described the dark patches on Mars as variations in vegetation. While the average temperature near the Martian equator was understood to be a bitterly cold -81°F (-63°C), temperatures could climb to a pleasant 68°F (20°C) during the Martian summer. Scientists theorized that at those times, cracks in rocks might retain this warmth long enough to support biological life.

In order to answer questions about life on Mars and to learn more about the planet, the US National Aeronautics and Space Administration (NASA) formed the Mariner program in 1962. On November 28, 1964,

NASA launched the *Mariner 4* spacecraft, which reached Mars on June 14, 1965. The craft flew 6,090 miles (9,800km) above the planet's southern hemisphere as a camera took 22 photographs. These photos, the first ever taken in deep space, were digitized by a primitive onboard computer and beamed back to Earth. The *Mariner 4* photographs showed Mars to be an ancient planet with large craters and no canals. Follow-up missions by *Mariner 6* and *Mariner 7* in 1969 provided another 200 photographs. These proved Mars was devoid of any large bodies of water or signs of

Mars (pictured) has been studied by scientists for decades as a possible host to some sort of alien life. Photos taken by several Mariner *spacecraft in the 1960s showed large craters but no canals and no large bodies of water or signs of life.*

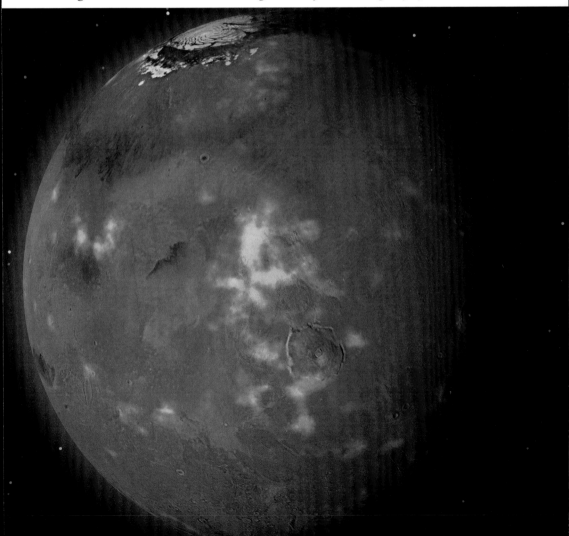

life. However, scientists continued to wonder if water might exist in the Martian soil or below the surface.

In 1971 new discoveries were made when *Mariner 9* went into orbit around Mars. When *Mariner* first arrived, the Martian surface was totally obscured by a huge dust storm, which lasted for several weeks. During this time *Mariner 9* photographed mini-tornadoes, commonly known as dust devils. These photos helped scientists finally understand that the dark red patches previously attributed to vegetation were actually swirling, blowing dust.

Fear of Lunar Bugs

In the late 1960s the discoveries made by the Mariner space probes were often overshadowed by NASA's Apollo missions. The program began in May 1961 when President John F. Kennedy told Congress the United States was committed to the goal "before this decade is out, of landing a man on the moon and returning him safely to the earth."[6] Americans achieved that goal on June 16, 1969, when *Apollo 11* astronauts, Neil Armstrong and Buzz Aldrin, became the first humans to walk on the lunar surface.

The Apollo moon landing inspired a national celebration, but when the astronauts returned to Earth, they were not given a parade. Instead they were quarantined in a tightly sealed trailer where they would not be in contact with other people or the environment. Chemistry professor Kevin W. Plaxco and science writer Michael Gross explain why the lunar visitors were isolated: "Heroes they may have been, but they would remain behind tightly sealed doors and windows as they, themselves, were some exotic Lunar samples. The reason? A fear of 'Lunar bugs' that might have infected them and could escape to wreak havoc on our planet."[7]

The men remained isolated for 17 days as scientists conducted experiments with the soil samples the astronauts had brought from the moon. Mice were exposed to the lunar dirt while scientists studied the gray dust under high-powered microscopes. After 17 days, no harmful pathogens had been found living in the dirt, and the astronauts finally received their celebratory parade in New York City.

The following December, two more astronauts visited the moon. When Peter Conrad and Alan Bean returned to Earth, they too were sent to the isolation trailer. No lunar microbes were found. While isolating the astronauts was a prudent step, most scientists did not expect any extraterrestrial contamination of Earth. As Plaxco and Gross explain, living organisms could not survive on the moon: "The argument against life on the Moon was and remains, basically, that if you wanted to build a really good sterilizer, you'd make something like the Moon's surface: no atmosphere, no water, extremes of heat well past the boiling point, intense radiation, and intense ultraviolet light [from the sun]."[8]

Searching for Water on Mars

The last manned lunar landing took place when *Apollo 17* touched down on the moon on December 7, 1972. By this time the fear of extraterrestrial microbes had subsided, and the astronauts were not required to spend time in the quarantine trailer when they returned. In the years that followed, NASA shifted its resources from landing astronauts on the moon to searching for biological life throughout the solar system.

In August and September 1975, NASA scientists launched a pair of identical space probes, *Viking 1* and *Viking 2*, on a journey to Mars. Each *Viking* spacecraft consisted of two parts, an orbiter and a lander. The orbiters contained video cameras and scientific instruments. According to NASA, the purpose of the equipment was to "obtain high resolution images of the Martian surface, characterize the structure and composition of the atmosphere and surface, and search for evidence of life."[9]

> **DID YOU KNOW?**
>
> Because of space constraints on the *Viking 1* lander, the equipment used to conduct complex tests for life on Mars had to fit into a box with a volume of 1 cubic foot (.3 cubic m) and a weight of less than 33 pounds (15kg).

Lunar soil samples, such as this one brought back from a 1971 moon mission, were isolated once on Earth to make sure any possible microorganisms did not escape and infect the planet.

Viking 1 touched down near the Martian equator in an area called the Chryse Planitia on June 26, 1976. Within a few minutes the lander began beaming information back to NASA, including the first color photo ever taken of the Martian surface. *Viking 2* touched down on September 3, 1976, in an area called Utopia Planitia near the polar ice cap. Signs of water in this region made it a favorable place to search for Martian life.

The necessity of water for life on other planets is explained by NASA scientist Peter Ward: "There can't be life in a solid, and there can't be life in a gas. In a gas, molecules are flying around so quickly that they can't carry out the complicated chemical reactions necessary for life. In a solid, they can barely move at all. Liquid is the [perfect] solvent for life: It's just right, allowing molecules to wiggle and slide past each other."[10]

Astrobiology and Alien Life

During its six years of operation, the *Viking 1* lander sent over 4,500 images of Mars back to Earth while its orbiter shot over 52,000 images. The lander also contained a compact biological laboratory designed to conduct three separate experiments meant to detect microbial life. The first experiment, called the labeled release (LR), was designed by Gilbert Levin.

Levin began his career as a sanitary engineer who invented a test to detect harmful bacteria in drinking water systems in California. He later became an astrobiologist, someone who investigates the possibilities of biological life developing on other planets. Astrobiologists study a wide variety of sciences including physics, chemistry, astronomy, biology, ecology, geography, and geology. This knowledge is used to develop theories about the origins, evolution, distribution, and future of life in the universe.

During Levin's LR experiment, the *Viking* lander dropped a liquid broth onto the Martian surface. The nutrients in the broth, playfully referred to by NASA scientists as chicken soup, were slightly radioactive. Scientists hoped microscopic bugs in the soil would eat the soup and exhale carbon dioxide, a gas humans and other animals exhale during the breathing process. If Martian bugs ate radioactive nutrients, the CO_2 they exhaled would be slightly radioactive. The radiation could be detected by an instrument on the lander called a Geiger counter.

The Geiger counter detected a rising level of radioactivity for several days after the addition of the broth to the soil. However, further additions of broth did not raise radiation levels. The results of the experiment were inconclusive, but in a 1997 book Levin stated his belief that "the Labeled Release experiment on [the] Viking Lander detected living organisms."[11]

Scientists continue to debate whether living organisms ate the *Viking* soup. The official NASA conclusion at the time was that no life exists on Mars, but the *Viking* found that "all elements essential to life on Earth—carbon, nitrogen, hydrogen, oxygen and phosphorus—were present on Mars."[12]

The Face on Mars

Most NASA scientists believed the *Viking* data finally proved that no sentient life existed on Mars. However, photos taken by the *Viking* orbiter spawned entirely new theories about advanced Martian civilizations and set off a wave of speculation not seen since the nineteenth century.

In 1977 Richard C. Hoagland examined a NASA photo of a mountain in the Cydonia region of Mars. He believed he saw a massive face carved into the Martian mountain. The image resembled the Great Sphinx in Egypt, which was carved around 2500 BC. Hoagland is a ufologist, or someone who studies reports of unidentified flying objects and space aliens. After observing the photo, Hoagland formulated the theory that the Face on Mars was part of a city built by an advanced civilization. Hoagland believes NASA knows about the extraterrestrials but is deliberately covering up the information because it would create widespread panic on Earth.

DID YOU KNOW?

Photographs taken by the Mars global surveyor in 2006 of two gullies on Mars revealed bright spots that suggest water might have flowed through them sometime during the previous seven years.

NASA called the Face on Mars a trick of light and shadow on the photographic images. But the story continued to attract interest. In 1982 two former NASA computer engineers, Vincent DePietro and Gregory Molenaar, used a computer to enhance photos of the huge mountain. This technique is controversial because the computer operator can enhance whatever features he or she wishes to reveal. After the enhancement, ufologists were able to see a clearer picture of the Face on Mars. It appears to be 1.6 miles (2.5km) long, 1.2 miles (2km) wide, and about 2,000 feet (610m) high. By 1986 more than a dozen books were written about the Face on Mars.

While researching the Face on Mars, ufologists claimed to have discovered several pyramid-like rocks about 7 miles (11.2km) away from the sphinxlike mountain. Some of these formations were said to be about 10 times the height of the Great Pyramid in Egypt, a towering 2,500 feet (762m) above the planet's surface. Australian science writer Brian Crowley believes the pyramid formations provide evidence of an extinct Martian civilization:

> [One] Mars pyramid teeters miraculously on the lip of a huge crater. There is no known explanation for how it might have got there. Other strange anomalies include what looks for all the world like a giant airport (or spaceport) with a central hub and wheel-like extensions, just like a modern airport. . . . There are also pockets of what could be underground tunnels—perhaps an underground network that collapsed.[13]

A Great Martian Flood

Some might dismiss fanciful descriptions of ancient Martian cities as science fiction. However, many astrobiologists believe that life might have existed on Mars millions or billions of years ago. As on Earth, geological features on Mars have evolved over the centuries. And some of the features mentioned by Crowley, such as the wheel-like valleys, might have been carved long ago by water during an era when the planet was warmer and more Earthlike. Astrobiologist Lewis Dartnell explains:

> [Photos of the Martian surface] clearly showed wide channels running down to the northern lowlands and great networks of valleys carving meanders [twists and bends] through the rough terrain of the highlands—looking for all the world like river courses on Earth. The prospects for flowing water on Mars, if

not today, then at least at some point in the past, were much more promising. Could the conditions on the young Mars have been much more [temperate], with a thicker atmosphere to better insulate the planet and provide conditions for liquid water?[14]

Dartnell based his observations on information provided by the Mars global surveyor. Launched in 1997, the global surveyor was equipped with a high-resolution digital camera capable of detecting much greater detail than the instruments used by the *Viking* orbiters. New images of Mars showed massive gorges surrounded by debris that spread out in fan-shaped patterns. The debris accumulations were similar to those created by flash flood gully washes in Earth's deserts.

The debris patterns provided evidence that water might once have been stored beneath a thick layer of Martian ice kept under intense pressure in underground reservoirs. Some event, such as a volcanic eruption or particularly warm season, could have melted the ice very quickly. This event would have released torrents of waters that contained carbon dioxide, a gas that makes bubbles in soda. Dartnell writes: "Once on the surface, dissolved carbon dioxide would instantly fizz out of [the water] solution as the pressure dropped, causing a spurting cascade to resemble the uncorking of an enormous bottle of champagne. . . . Some calculations show that a single torrent could unleash up to a billion cubic meters of water a second."[15]

Such an event would have had a destructive power hundreds of times greater than the largest flashflood ever recorded on Earth. It would have quickly reshaped the planet's surface, creating vast oceans in the northern lowland region. Evidence of a mass meltdown can be seen in photographs of the lowlands where contours in the land appear to be shorelines and beaches created by ancient oceans. Some astrobiologists even speculate that a great Martian flood might have occurred as recently as the early

A 1976 Viking *orbiter photograph of Mars shows a huge rock formation (center) that resembles a human head. Shadows give the illusion of eyes, nose, and a mouth. After seeing this photo, a prominent ufologist suggested the "face" was part of a city built by an advanced civilization.*

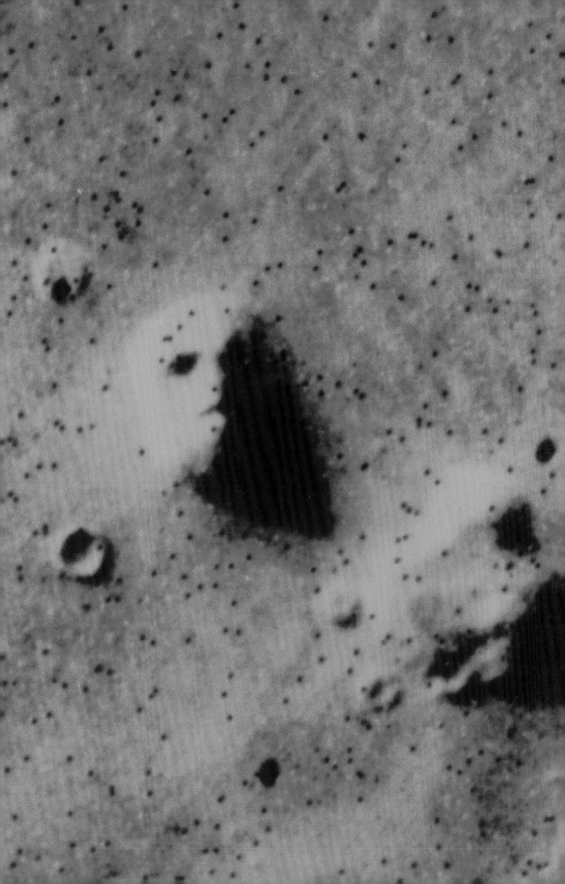

eighteenth century. But whether the pools of water, no matter how large, could have allowed microscopic life to gain a foothold on Mars remains a mystery.

Martian Meteorites

Some of the best evidence of life on Mars has not come from space probes but from evidence found on Earth. In 1980 a 17.4-pound meteorite (7.9kg) was found in Antarctica with a chemical makeup that distinguished it from other typical meteorites. Meteorites are rocks from outer space that survive impact with Earth or another planet. Most of these objects, which can be as small as a grain of sand or as large as a boulder, begin life as space debris traveling through the solar system.

Scientists determined the Antarctica meteorite, named EETA79001, has a chemical makeup similar to Martian rocks that had been analyzed by the *Viking* experiments. With this discovery, scientists began examining the 24,000 meteorites that have been collected around the world during the past 200 years. In 1993 it became clear for the first time that about 34 of these meteorites originated on Mars. They were likely launched into space about 15 million years ago when a huge meteorite collided with Mars. The collision pushed massive clouds of rocks and debris into outer space, and some of it headed toward Earth. About 13,000 years ago a tiny portion of these rocks landed in Antarctica where they were buried in ice and snow. Over time, a few of the Martian meteorites were discovered by explorers.

> **DID YOU KNOW?**
>
> The microscopic fossils found in the Martian meteorite labeled ALH84001 are about 1/1000 the thickness of a human hair.

In 1994 a team of planetary scientists at the Johnson Space Center in Houston began examining another Martian meteorite labeled ALH84001. It was originally discovered in Antarctica in 1984. After a two-year investigation, the team, headed by David McKay, Everett

Martian Volcanoes

Astrobiologist Lewis Dartnell explains how volcanoes once made Mars warm and watery and how their demise turned the planet into a lifeless rock:

> [The] Martian atmosphere is extremely thin but in primordial times, soon after the formation of both Mars and Earth, it is thought they were cloaked in similar atmospheres. Carbon dioxide, methane and water vapor in the air would have provided an appreciable greenhouse effect, [warming] and insulating the young planets. . . . To achieve the conditions to permit liquid water, Mars probably would have needed an atmosphere several times thicker than the current terrestrial blanket; it is further out than Earth and, in those days, the Sun was also around twenty-five percent dimmer. Much of this atmosphere would have been [created] by the huge Martian volcanoes, driven by heat stored within the planet's interior.
>
> . . . [Each volcanic] eruption might have released enough carbon dioxide for a slightly increased greenhouse effect, providing a brief spell of warmer conditions. But over time, the heat reserved within Mars dwindled and volcanic activity steadily diminished. The planet was dying inside and the eruptions replenishing the atmosphere with vital [warming] gases became less and less frequent.
>
> . . . Our own planet will suffer the same fate in perhaps another billion years.

Lewis Dartnell, *Life in the Universe*. Oxford: OneWorld, 2007, pp. 121–22.

Gibson, and Kathie Thomas-Keprta, shocked the world. According to McKay, the meteorite showed "evidence of past life on Mars . . . [including a] unique pattern of organic molecules, carbon compounds that are the basis of life. We also found several unusual mineral phases that are known products of primitive microscopic organisms on Earth."[16] The presence of what appeared to be microscopic fossils support this startling announcement. However, ALH84001 appeared to be 3.6 billion years old, and scientists are unsure whether life even existed on Earth at that time. Whatever the case, the meteorites allowed scientists to study actual rocks from the red planet while trying to piece together the puzzle of life on Mars.

While there are no sentient beings on Mars, the study of Martian meteorites might lead to the conclusion that microscopic life exists in the solar system, as science writer Charles Schmidt explains:

> If your idea of a Martian is a little green man who hops out of a UFO . . . you're probably in for a disappointment. A real Martian, should it exist, might resemble a tiny microbe sustained by minimal, intermittent water supplies and the energy . . . [generated by] hydrogen and carbon dioxide. If you saw a Martian colony at home, you'd probably try to wipe it off the counter with Formula 409 [cleaning] spray.[17]

Changing Views

Scientific views of Mars changed considerably during the twentieth and twenty-first centuries. In the early 1900s, some astronomers were convinced that sentient beings dug canals on Mars. In the 1970s, findings by NASA space probes suggested that water—long since frozen—might have created canals as it flowed across the planet in the distant past. By the 1990s, scientists had come to believe that water somewhere beneath the planet's surface might support forms of microscopic life. No one can as yet say for certain whether life exists—or has ever existed—on Mars but the robotic rovers continue to dig in the Martian dirt for clues.

CHAPTER TWO

Space Probes, Chemicals, and Microbes

In 1610 Italian astronomer Galileo Galilei discovered four moons circling Jupiter. He named the moons Europa, Io, Ganymede, and Callisto, after mythical women who were lovers of the Greek god Zeus. In the centuries following Galileo's discovery, another 59 moons were found to be circling Jupiter, the fifth planet from the sun and the largest in the solar system.

In the era of modern space exploration, Europa, which is slightly smaller than Earth's moon, has been the focus of intense study. In 1996 the unmanned *Galileo* spacecraft, named after the famous astronomer, beamed photographs of Europa back to Earth. The pictures showed the moon to be a unique world unto itself. Europa's surface is made entirely of ice frozen to -260°F (-126°C). The discovery of ice gave rise to the speculation that a deep ocean may exist beneath the ice. Planetary scientists believe this body of water might be 50 to 100 miles (80km to 160km) deep, which would make it the largest ocean in the solar system. In theory, marine life such as microbes, anemones, and tiny fish, could live in the waters beneath the frozen surface of Europa's ocean.

NASA hopes to further explore the possibility of water and extraterrestrial life on the Jovian moon with its Europa Jupiter System Mission

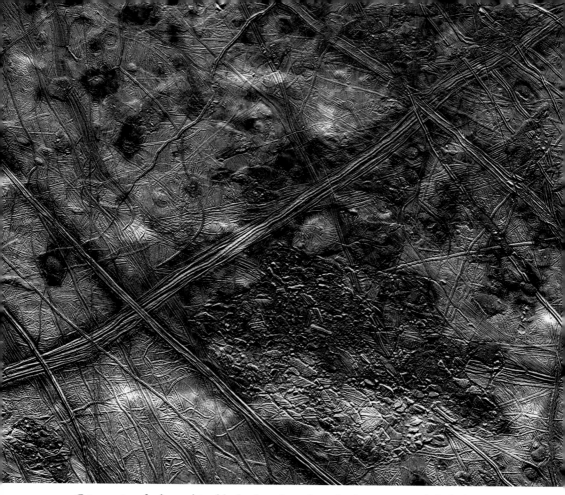

Crisscrossing faults and ice blocks thought to have broken apart and shifted can be seen in this photograph of the surface of Europa, one of Jupiter's moons. Scientists believe that a deep ocean may exist beneath the moon's icy surface.

(EJSM). If plans go forward with the EJSM, a spacecraft will circle Europa in 2038 gathering information; a lander will follow 10 to 20 years later. The objective of the EJSM is to determine if Europa hosts sub-ice oceans or other environments that would be conducive to life.

Evolution on Earth

If life exists on Europa or other nearby planets, astrobiologists say, evolution is likely to have played a large role in its development. This belief is modeled on the way all living organisms on Earth evolved over the past 3.5 billion years.

Evolution was first described by English naturalist Charles Darwin in 1854. According to Darwin, the physical traits common to a population of organisms can change over time. This allows one species to evolve into another species. Since Darwin's time, countless experiments, observations, and evaluations have proved that living organisms evolved naturally over billons of years. The process is thought to have begun when simple organic life-forms came into existence as chemical compounds in the atmosphere. These compounds were exposed to lightning or some other natural forces which gave them life. As Darwin speculated, the first living organisms emerged in "some warm little pond, with all sorts of ammonia and phosphoric salts, light, heat, electricity, etc."[18]

Stellar Evolution

Darwin's theory of biological evolution says all organisms arose from a common ancestry. Astrobiologists use this concept to imagine evolution on other planets in a theory called stellar evolution. Stellar evolution is based on the idea that all matter in the universe, from Earth's solar system to the billions of galaxies beyond, has a common origin. They were blasted into existence during a process called the Big Bang, which gave birth to everything that exists in the universe.

The Big Bang formed trillions of stars in a process that also created a nearly infinite amount of organic chemicals, called biogenic elements. Major biogenic elements include carbon, nitrogen, helium, hydrogen, oxygen, sulfur, and phosphorus. These organic chemicals are present in stars, planets, meteors, and other elements of the universe. Molecules of these elements are also found in living organisms on Earth.

Collecting Stardust

During the Big Bang biogenic elements were propelled throughout the universe. Gases such as hydrogen gathered in huge clouds and ignited, forming massive stars, some that are hundreds of times bigger than the sun. When the stars formed, heat-resistant granules containing biogenic elements were ejected into the universe. These granules are called presolar grains or, more commonly, stardust. The chemical-laden stardust, older

The Big Bang Forms the Universe

Scientific experiments have determined that the Big Bang occurred about 13.7 billion years ago. One-millionth of a second after the bang, everything in the universe, all matter and energy, was compacted into an unimaginably hot, dense plasma. Several minutes into the explosion, basic elements such as hydrogen and helium were formed as temperatures cooled.

For about 1 billion years after the Big Bang, temperatures fell, allowing the formation of countless hydrogen and helium gas clouds. Some of these gas clouds ignited into giant red stars called supernova. These stars are more than 10 times the size of the sun. The red giants were characterized by extreme pressure and high heat which caused massive explosions. These conditions forged chemical molecules such as carbon, oxygen, nitrogen, iron, nickel, and other biogenic elements. The extremely hot chemicals were propelled away from the red giant stars that created them. The elements cooled and bonded into small bodies similar to asteroids and comets. Billions of these were pulled together by gravitational forces around stars and eventually grew into planets. Some of the chemical elements, however, remained in a gaseous state and formed planets like Jupiter, Saturn, Uranus, and Neptune. These so-called gas planets are composed largely of hydrogen, helium, methane, and ammonia.

than Earth itself, continues to travel through interstellar space, pulled along in the tails of comets.

Scientists have long believed that the stardust chemicals in comets work like seeds. As comets travel throughout the universe, they distribute the life-giving elements to planets, asteroids, and moons. These elements are thought to be responsible for the beginnings of life on Earth and, possibly, other planets in the universe.

In order to determine the importance of stardust, NASA launched the *Stardust* spacecraft in 1999. *Stardust* traveled 1.5 billion miles through the solar system to rendezvous with the tail of a comet named Wild-2 on

January 2, 2004. The spacecraft was outfitted with a special collection grid filled with a spongelike material. The grid captured samples of gas and dust from the tail of the Wild-2 comet. The material, the first ever retrieved from a comet, was stored in a special canister. When *Stardust* passed into Earth's orbit on January 15, 2006, the canister, which was attached to a parachute, was ejected from the spacecraft. The canister full of stardust came back to Earth at the Utah Test and Training Range about 80 miles (130km) west of Salt Lake City.

The Ingredients of Life

The stardust specimens collected from Wild-2 were so tiny they were measured in billionths of a gram. Researchers spent two years developing equipment sensitive enough to test the material, but the results were exciting: The tail of Wild-2 contained the amino acid glycine, one of the building blocks of life. Astrobiologist Jamie Elsila of NASA's Goddard Space Flight Center explains the importance of this discovery: "Glycine is . . . used by living organisms to make proteins, and this is the first time an amino acid has been found in a comet. Our discovery supports the theory that some of life's ingredients formed in space and were delivered to Earth long ago by meteorite and comet impacts."[19]

> **DID YOU KNOW?**
>
> When the *Deep Impact* probe collided with Tempel 1, the comet was traveling through space at 23,000 miles per hour (37,000kmh).

Glycine is found in the tissues and cells of plants and in animals. In humans, glycine plays a major role in the synthesis of proteins and is found in the spinal cord where it aids in the function of the central nervous system.

The *Stardust* mission helped astrobiologists establish proof for what many have long suspected, according to Carl Pilcher, director of the NASA Astrobiology Institute: "The discovery of glycine in a comet supports the idea that the fundamental building blocks of life are prevalent in space, and strengthens the argument that life in the universe may be common rather than rare."[20]

Deep Impact

After *Stardust* released its canister above the skies of Utah, mission scientists sent it back into deep space to collect samples from the comet Tempel 1. This mission marked NASA's second visit to Tempel 1. The initial exploration of the comet occurred on July 3, 2005, when Tempel 1 passed within 83 million miles (133 million km) of Earth. At that time, the *Deep Impact* spacecraft released a 770-pound probe (349kg) to crashland on Tempel 1.

When the *Deep Impact* probe collided with the comet, it blasted a large crater 70 feet (21m) deep and 300 feet (91.4m) wide into the surface. Cameras on *Deep Impact* took thousands of photographs of flying debris created by the impact. In October 2006 scientists studying the pictures announced that Tempel 1 has three small areas covered with ice. *Deep Impact* investigator Jessica Sunshine explains the significance of this discovery: "[This] is the first evidence of water ice on comets. Understanding a comet's water cycle and supply is critical to understanding these bodies as a . . . possible source that delivered water to Earth. Add the large organic [chemical] component in comets and you have two of the key ingredients for life."[21]

The Methane Lakes of Titan

Astrobiologists understand that water is a crucial element for life. On Earth, water supports life in oceans, lakes, and rivers and even in the driest deserts. But scientists speculate other liquids besides water could support alien life on other planets. For example, exotic life might evolve in the liquid ammonia clouds that flow in abundance on Jupiter or the liquid sulfuric acid that blankets Venus. For this reason, some scientists feel the search for alien life should move beyond the hunt for water. As molecular biologist Steven Benner asks, "How do you know this 'follow the water' strategy isn't going to miss the weirder forms of life that don't require water?"[22]

Benner's question might be answered by space probes to Titan, the largest of 30 moons circling Saturn. Titan is about 50 percent larger than Earth's moon. It was first observed by Dutch astronomer Christian Huygens in 1655, but little was known about Titan until the twentieth century. In 1907 the Spanish astronomer Josep Comas i Sola was observing the distant satellite through a powerful telescope when he noticed a phenomenon called limb darkening. When a planet or moon exhibits limb darkening the edges appears darker than the center. Limb darkening indicates the presence of an atmosphere, a layer of gases held in place by gravity. In 1944 scientific observations showed that Titan did indeed have a fully developed atmosphere, akin to the one that blankets Earth.

In the 1970s scientists were able to determine that Titan's atmosphere is largely composed of nitrogen and methane. On Earth, methane is the main component of natural gas and is found in petroleum. The gas is also produced by decomposing garbage, animal waste, and plant life. Methane is called a hydrocarbon because it is composed of carbon and hydrogen molecules. The substance makes up an extremely tiny portion of Earth's atmosphere, 0.00017 percent. Saturn's atmosphere contains a much greater concentration of methane, about 0.4 percent. And the presence of methane in Titan's atmosphere is relatively high, at 1.6 percent. It has created thousands of liquid methane lakes on Titan, with an estimated average depth of 140 feet (42.6m). These are the only large, stable bodies of surface liquid known to exist anywhere besides on Earth.

A Frozen Version of an Ancient Earth

Titan is 9.5 times further away from the sun than is Earth. At this distance it receives little more than 1 percent of the solar energy received by

Earth. This makes Titan a very cold place, with temperatures averaging –290° F (–179° C).

Despite the extreme temperatures, the presence of an atmosphere and large bodies of liquid make Titan the most Earthlike world ever found in the solar system. That does not mean it resembles present-day Earth, however. NASA science writer Enrico Piazza explains: "With its thick atmosphere and organic-rich chemistry, Titan resembles a frozen version of Earth, several billion years ago, before life began pumping oxygen into our atmosphere."[23]

The surface features of Titan remained unexplored until the early twenty-first century because its atmosphere produces a dense smog. This methane and hydrogen brew, which give Titan its famed orange color, is chemically similar to the smog that hangs over many large cities on Earth, but it is much thicker. To penetrate Titan's atmosphere, NASA launched the spacecraft *Cassini-Huygens* in 1997, in partnership with the European Space Agency (ESA).

> ### DID YOU KNOW?
>
> It took the *Huygens* probe more than seven years to travel to Saturn's moon Titan, where the probe transmitted information back to Earth for less than two hours.

The robotic *Cassini-Huygens* spacecraft consisted of two parts, the *Cassini* orbiter and the *Huygens* probe. When the spacecraft reached Titan in 2004, *Cassini* began beaming photographs back to Earth. The pictures revealed for the first time Titan's methane lakes that ebb and flow and perform "complex, Earth-like processes that shape [Titan's] surface,"[24] according to Piazza. *Cassini* revealed features including shorelines, riverbeds, and canyons—all sculpted by liquid methane.

On January 14, 2005, the small, battery-powered *Huygens* probe descended on a parachute into Titan's atmosphere and landed on the surface. This was the first landing to ever take place in the outer solar system, and the probe touched down in a substance with the texture of wet sand. Upon landing, *Huygens* began sending pictures back to Earth.

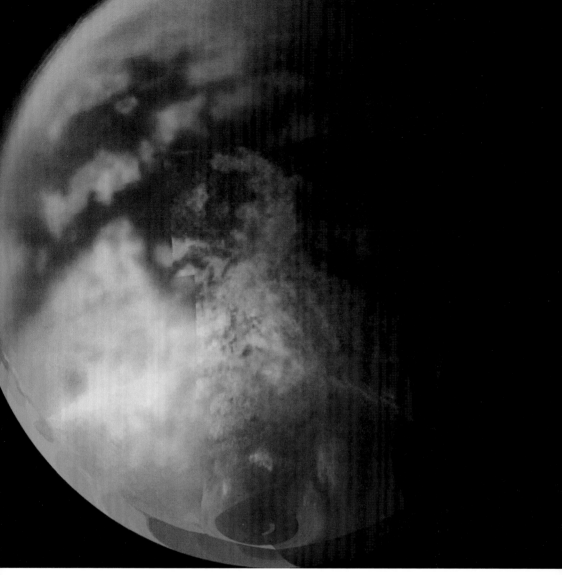

The surface of Saturn's largest moon, Titan, can be seen in this combined infrared and optical image taken by the Cassini *orbiter. The* Cassini *images revealed shorelines, riverbeds, and canyons—all sculpted by liquid methane.*

These photos revealed a landscape shaped by liquid methane that cycles in a manner similar to the way water moves on Earth. Astrobiologist Lewis Dartnell explains how this process works:

> Methane evaporates, saturating the air to form clouds that become laden and soon begin raining on the highlands. The liquid methane runs downhill towards the plains, coursing along

the river valleys, picking up sediment, transporting rocks and smoothing them off, then pooling into shallow lakes before soaking into the ground. The interpretation is that the surface of Titan is like crème brulée; beneath a thin hard crust the ground is sodden with liquid methane.[25]

Methane-Based Life

The question of whether living creatures could evolve in a methane-based atmosphere is a point of research for astrobiologists working on the *Cassini* mission. Scientists suggest that life might exist on Titan in the form of creatures that use liquid methane to form cells and other biological structures in the same way organisms on Earth use water. These creatures would form methane-based life as opposed to the familiar water-based life of Earth.

In 2005 NASA astrobiologist Chris McKay named Titan's theoretical methane-based creatures "methanogens." Instead of breathing oxygen the methanogens would breathe or otherwise consume methane or hydrogen in Titan's atmosphere. They might also consume other hydrocarbon chemicals found on Titan, such as acetylene and ethane.

After its first visit to Titan the *Cassini* spacecraft continued with its mission, photographing and conducting experiments over Saturn and its other moons. In 2010 the spacecraft made another pass over Titan and provided new information about the possible existence of methanogens. Using various chemicals on Titan, astrobiologists developed a complex theory of how methane-based life might form.

Before *Cassini*'s second pass over Titan, scientists believed hydrogen would be evenly distributed in the upper and lower regions of the atmo-

> ### DID YOU KNOW?
>
> NASA reported in September 2010 that the *Cassini* spacecraft had traveled 2.6 billion miles, orbited Saturn 125 times, conducted 67 flybys of Titan, 8 flybys of the icy moon Enceladus, and taken a total of 210,000 photographs.

Water Geysers on Enceladus

Titan is not the only Saturnian moon of interest to astrobiologists. Enceladus, the sixth-largest moon of Saturn, is about one-quarter the size of Titan. Enceladus is covered in water ice that reflects sunlight, making the moon one of the brightest objects in the solar system. However, Enceladus is extremely cold, with average surface temperatures around -324°F (-162°C).

Enceladus came to the attention of NASA scientists in 2005 when a *Cassini* flyby detected a giant plume of water ice spraying from cracks in the moon's surface. On another flyby in November 2009, *Cassini* photographed 30 of these cloudy, white geysers, referred to by astronomers as tiger stripes. Analysis shows the water is salty, which provides evidence that a large ocean exists under the frozen surface of Enceladus. Some of this salty water spray might be responsible for the icy rings that encircle Saturn.

sphere, and equally present near the ground. However, *Cassini* showed that hydrogen, abundant in Titan's upper atmosphere, seems to be lacking near the surface. NASA scientist Darrell Strobel comments on this phenomenon, "It's as if you have a hose and you're squirting hydrogen onto the ground, but it's disappearing."[26]

The lack of hydrogen is only part of the mystery. The hydrocarbon acetylene is also in short supply. Scientists believe that Titan's atmosphere should be producing an abundance of acetylene when the sun's rays hit the methane atmosphere. However, acetylene is only present in small quantities. This leads some astrobiologists to conclude that methanogens are eating the acetylene produced by the atmosphere. They are also breathing hydrogen near the surface, leaving lower levels of the gas than would be expected. According to McKay, "We suggested hydrogen consumption [among methanogens] because it's the obvious gas for life to consume on Titan, similar to the way we consume oxygen on Earth. If these signs do turn out to be a sign of life, it would be doubly exciting because it would represent a . . . form of life independent from water-based life on Earth."[27]

"Really Alien Life"

Researchers at the University of Arizona have conducted complex chemical experiments to test the possibility of methane-based life evolving on Titan. They mixed methane, nitrogen, and carbon monoxide to mimic the main ingredients of Titan's atmosphere. The chemicals were then frozen and exposed to ultraviolet radiation to imitate the sun's rays. During the experiment, the chemical bonds of the nitrogen were broken, which produced over 20,000 different molecules. These included the amino acids glycine and alanine. The experiment also created the four most basic components found in the cells of living creatures: cytosine, adenine, thymine, and guanine.

These molecules had been produced from water in previous experiments studying primitive life. The Arizona experiment was unique because it was the first time the molecules were synthesized without water. Researcher Sarah Horst comments on the results, "We don't need liquid water. . . . We show that it is possible to make very complex molecules in the outer parts of an atmosphere."[28]

The Arizona experiment illustrates how complex molecules could form in a nitrogen-rich atmosphere like Titan's and create a basic form of life. It may also offer insight into the way life emerged on Earth. Life possibly emerged high in the atmosphere rather than forming in a chemical-filled swamp. Whatever the case, Saturn's biggest moon remains a central focus for astrobiologists like Peter Ward, who states, "Titan is so cool. Titan is the most exciting place in the solar system astrobiologically. It has the most exciting chemistry set in our solar system by far. If there's life on Titan, it's alien life—really alien life."[29]

Goldilocks Planets

Titan might be the prime location in the solar system for astrobiological activity. But the galaxy contains hundreds of billions of sun-like stars. Many of these stars have planets, called exoplanets, in their orbits. By 2010 astronomers had observed 496 known exoplanets with hundreds more awaiting confirmation. Those who study exoplanets believe that some of these worlds might have Earthlike environmental conditions in which humanlike creatures could evolve. Other exoplanets might host exotic life-forms that consume methane or some biogenic element.

Of all the exoplanets, the one that has generated the most excitement is known as Gliese 581g, which was discovered in September 2010. This is the fourth planet circling the star Gliese 581, which lies 20.5 light-years, or 119 trillion miles (192 trillion km) from Earth. Located in the constellation Libra, Gliese 581 is much smaller than the sun and is called a red dwarf star. Red dwarfs, which make up the majority of stars in the universe, are those that are less than half the mass of the sun and generate about 10 percent of the luminosity, or radiant heat and light.

Although Gliese 581 is one-third the mass of the sun, the exoplanet Gliese 581g is about 4.5 times bigger than Earth. This "super-Earth," as it is called, orbits its dim sun at a distance of about 14 million miles (22 million km). This puts Gliese 581g in what is called a habitable zone, one that might have a climate which could provide liquid water and host extraterrestrial life. Alien worlds in habitable zones are called Goldilocks planets by astronomers. This name is taken from the fairy tale "Goldilocks and the Three Bears" in which a girl named Goldilocks chooses porridge that is not too hot or not too cold, but just right. The orbit of a Goldilocks planet around a star is thought to be just right for alien life.

Astrobiologists have not been able to determine if biological life exists on Gliese 581g. However, astronomer Steven S. Vogt, who led the team that discovered Gliese 581g states, "This is the first exoplanet that has the right conditions for water to exist on its surface . . . [the] chances of life on this planet are almost 100 percent."[30] While Vogt remains confident that Gliese 581g is a Goldilocks planet, not all scientists are convinced.

Because of its great distance from Earth, no one can be 100 percent sure that life exists near a star in the Libra constellation.

Close to Home

While the hunt for intelligent beings on Gliese 581g and other exoplanets persists, the most promising prospects for alien life are closer to home. The *Cassini* spacecraft will continue to orbit Saturn and Titan until it ends in a fiery crash on Saturn's surface in 2017. Meanwhile, the space probe sends new information to NASA every day. Whether microscopic methane eaters will ever be discovered thriving on moons or planets in Earth's solar system remains to be seen.

CHAPTER THREE

Scanning the Skies for Intelligent Life

Between 2005 and 2010, astronomers at the W.M. Keck Observatory in Hawaii analyzed thousands of distant stars. The scientists were searching for two specific types of movement that would signal the presence of life-supporting planets. Each star was analyzed for a telltale wobble that is caused by gravity when a planet orbits a star. Astronomers were also looking for a slight dimming when an exoplanet passed in front of its sun.

After five years of exacting work, Keck astronomers discovered 166 stars with Earthlike exoplanets in their orbit. The distant planets were orbiting habitable zones. The Keck study provided information that allowed astronomers to estimate that at least 46 billion Goldilocks planets are in the Milky Way galaxy—planets that are not too hot and not too cold but just right for life to exist. As lead astronomer on the Keck project Andrew Howard comments, "In our galaxy [Earthlike planets] are like grains of sand sprinkled on a beach—they are everywhere."[31]

Active and Passive Searches

The Keck Observatory, located at the summit of Hawaii's Mauna Kea volcano, has two of the most powerful and precise telescopes in the world. But even these high-tech instruments cannot determine if intelligent beings exist on distant exoplanets. Since traveling trillions of miles in a spacecraft is impossible, scientists from various fields of study have devised other ways of scouring the universe in search of sentient beings.

One program searches for signals from alien societies, while the other sends messages into space. The program called Search for Extraterrestrial Intelligence (SETI) scans the skies seeking radio frequency signals produced by civilizations on distant planets. SETI is a passive approach to interstellar contact. If a signal is ever received from another planet, humans are not obligated to respond. In such a case, humanity would know of the existence of another intelligent life-form but the aliens would not know if life existed on Earth. The program called Communications with Extraterrestrial Intelligence (CETI) involves sending specially prepared signals into space hoping they are received and decoded by an alien race. Some scientists believe this active search, which would announce the presence of the human race to extraterrestrials, is risky. The risks of alien contact were discussed in April 2010 by renowned British physicist Stephen Hawking. Hawking believes that intelligent life probably exists on distant planets, but he warns that extraterrestrials might be extremely hostile to humans:

> **DID YOU KNOW?**
>
> Each telescope at the Keck Observatory is 80 feet (24m) high, 32 feet (10m) in diameter, and weighs 600,000 pounds (272,115kg).

We only have to look at ourselves to see how intelligent life might develop into something we wouldn't want to meet. I imagine they might exist in massive ships, having used up all the resources from their home planet. Such advanced aliens would perhaps become nomads, looking to conquer and colonize whatever planets they can reach. . . . I think the outcome would be much as when Christopher Columbus first landed in America, which didn't turn out very well for the Native Americans.[32]

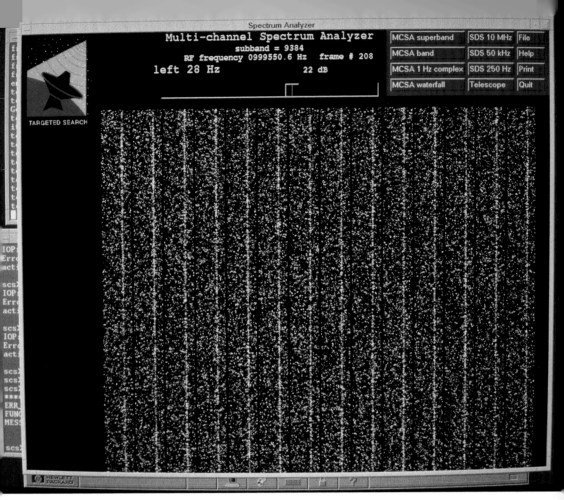

A test signal from the world's largest and most sensitive radio telescope, the Arecibo Observatory in Puerto Rico, shows on a computer screen. Arecibo is one of the radio telescopes that searches for signals from extraterrestrial civilizations.

Radio Waves

Radio telescopes have been used since 1960 in the search for intelligent life in the universe. Radio telescopes are directional antennas that can both receive and broadcast radio waves. The most familiar type of radio telescope has a dish-shaped antenna that receives incoming radio waves. That information is fed through a smaller antenna to a computer for analysis.

Scientists believe that the electromagnetic signals generated by radio waves on Earth might be intercepted by alien civilizations. These long-lasting waves, called artifact signals, might also be produced by extraterrestrial civilizations. If so, scientists known as radio astronomers would be able to pick up the signals.

Radio telescopes support both SETI and CETI activities. Scientists search for intelligent life by listening for faint electromagnetic waves that might be produced on other planets. They also beam specially prepared messages aimed at specific portions of the galaxy where Earthlike exoplanets might be circling distant suns.

"A Channel of Communication"

During more than 60 years of SETI research, no artifact signals have been received. In the early days of SETI, however, some scientists were certain that radio astronomy would answer basic questions about life in the universe. This confidence was evident in the September 19, 1959, issue of *Nature*, in an article called "Searching for Interstellar Communications" by physicists Giuseppe Cocconi and Philip Morrison:

> [Near] some star rather like the Sun there are civilizations with scientific interests and with technical possibilities much greater than those now available to us. . . . It is highly probable that for a long time they will have been expecting the development of science near [our] Sun. We shall assume that long ago they established a channel of communication that would one day become known to us, and that they look forward patiently to the answering signals from [us] which would make known to them that a new society has entered the community of intelligence.[33]

Project Ozma

The *Nature* article concludes that the "probability of success is difficult to estimate, but if we never search the chance of success is zero."[34] About eight months after the article was published astronomer Frank Drake conducted the first SETI project, using equipment at the National Radio Astronomy Observatory at Green Bank, WV. In a pioneering experiment called Project Ozma, the 30-year-old Drake aimed a radio telescope at the stars Epsilon Eridani and Tau Ceti, 10.5 and 12 light-years from Earth, respectively. Although both stars were relatively close to Earth and were suspected of hosting Goldilocks planets, no artifact electromagnetic waves were detected from those areas of space.

Project Ozma failed in its mission, but Drake managed to keep interest in SETI alive by devising what is called the Drake equation. First published in 1965, the equation uses a complex mathematical formula that considers the number of stars and the possible number of planets orbiting those stars. By factoring in variables, such as the number of planets in habitable zones, Drake concluded that at least 10,000 planets in the Milky Way host intelligent life and that beings on these planets would be capable of communicating with or traveling to Earth.

Drake based his equation on the mediocrity principle. The term mediocre, while often used to denote something that is of poor quality, also means commonplace. The mediocrity principle is based on the idea that

Project Cyclops

In 1971 NASA initiated an ambitious project to search for intelligent life up to 1,000 light-years from Earth. The objective of Project Cyclops was to initiate a program using "state-of-the-art techniques aimed at detecting the existence of extraterrestrial intelligent life."

Project Cyclops was named after the one-eyed giants of Greek mythology. The program's one giant eye was planned as an array of 1,000 individual 328-foot steerable parabolic dish antennas (100m). The 1,000-unit matrix was to be arranged in a hexagonal (6-sided) pattern about 23 square miles (60 square km) in diameter. The Cyclops matrix would act as a single giant radio antenna searching the universe for extraterrestrial signals. The project's estimated cost at the time was more than $10 billion—which was $10 billion more than Congress wanted to spend. The project was shelved. Radio astronomers hoped to build a similar antenna matrix on the dark side of the moon, but this project was also canceled.

Quoted in Ronald D. Ekers et al., eds., *SETI 2020*. Mountain View, CA: SETI, 2002, p. 20.

the conditions that support life on Earth are commonplace in the universe. As Drake stated in a 2010 interview, "what happened in [our] Solar System was not unusual. It did not require any special circumstances, or any freak situations, and therefore what happened [on Earth] should have happened in many places, and that includes the evolution of an intelligent technology-using creature."[35]

The Fermi Paradox

Not every scientist agrees with the Drake equation or the mediocrity principle. Skeptics promote a theory known as the Fermi paradox, devised by physicist Enrico Fermi in 1950. When discussing extraterrestrials, Fermi asked why no other advanced civilization besides Earth's population ever arose on the billions of planets in the Milky Way.

The universe is billions of years old, Fermi noted. Surely, he concluded, if intelligent beings existed somewhere in the universe they would have devised methods for interstellar travel at some point during that long period of time. Theoretically, advanced aliens could have colonized one planet, and after a few thousand years their descendents could have set off to colonize another planet. According to Fermi's calculations, this advanced race of space beings might have visited every habitable planet in the entire Milky Way galaxy within 50 million years. While 50 million years is a long time by human standards, it is only about 1 percent of the age of the Milky Way. Since aliens have not colonized the Milky Way, Fermi asked, "Where is everybody?"[36] The galaxy does not appear to teem with life, and no credible reports by earthlings of visitations or communications with alien races have surfaced. The Fermi paradox asks, if humans are not alone, where are the others?

A Matrix of Radio Telescopes

Debate on the question of whether intelligent beings could possibly inhabit a planet somewhere in the universe has continued over the years. In 1967 two British astrophysicists, Jocelyn Bell Burnell and Antony Hewish, caused a stir when they recorded unusually rhythmic radio signals coming from a celestial object. At first the scientists humorously called the odd pulsating signal the "little green men" or LGM signal, indicating it might be produced by extraterrestrials. Subsequent study showed the signal was from a natural source, a young pulsating star called a pulsar. The pair later shared the Nobel Prize for physics for their discovery.

Although alien radio signals remained elusive, interest in SETI remained high at NASA. In 1971 scientists at the space agency proposed building a massive array, or matrix, of radio telescopes that would be wired together. This powerful array could search for signals up to 1,000 light-years from Earth. The program, called Project Cyclops, would have cost the equivalent of $53 billion. Even in an era when astronauts were walking on the moon, Project Cyclops was deemed too expensive, and the array of radio telescopes was never constructed. However, the ambitious design study for Project Cyclops inspired a generation of SETI researchers. In 2002 astronomer Ronald D. Ekers praised the concept: "Those who read the [Project Cyclops] report today often remark on both the clarity of the analysis and on how much of it is still [relevant], nearly three decades later."[37]

Despite such praise, the decade of the 1970s was an era of cost-cutting at NASA. Powerful politicians whose committees funded various space programs believed SETI was a waste of tax dollars. With a budget of less than $1 million for SETI programs, radio astronomers focused on low-cost, targeted research of nearby stars. Rather than scan the entire universe with a massive antennae matrix, they used radio telescopes already in place.

The Pictorial Plaque

Even as government funding for SETI decreased, NASA scientists took an active role in trying to initiate contact with alien civilizations. Since the 1970s three CETI projects have been designed with the intent of sending greetings to extraterrestrials.

The first CETI project was *Pioneer 10*, launched in March 1972 to photograph Jupiter and its moons and conduct scientific tests in the Jovian system. After conducting its mission, *Pioneer 10* continued to travel through space, passing distant Neptune in 1983 and moving out of the solar system not long after. The small robotic spacecraft is aimed at a red star called Aldebaran, which forms the eye of the constellation Taurus (the Bull), 68 light-years from Earth. *Pioneer 10* will not reach Aldebaran for about 2 million years. If the journey is completed, intelligent beings living on Goldilocks planets near that distant star might receive a message from Earth written in 1972. The spacecraft is carrying what is called the Pioneer plaque, a pictorial message to aliens from humanity.

The Pioneer plaque is a sheet of gold-anodized aluminum plate measuring 6 inches by 9 inches (15.2cm by 22.9cm). It contains engraved images and symbols designed for NASA by Drake and renowned astrophysicist Carl Sagan. The artwork was prepared by Sagan's wife at the time, Linda Salzman Sagan. Several symbols on the Pioneer plaque are believed to be universal and would therefore be understood by advanced beings on distant exoplanets. For example, the plaque includes a picture of the hydrogen molecule, the most abundant element in the universe. Figures of an unclothed man and woman are engraved on the plaque. The man is holding his hand up in a gesture of greeting. While this might not be understood by aliens, it shows the hand, fingers, and thumb and the manner in which people move their arms. A silhouette of *Pioneer* is shown behind the figures to indicate the average size of human beings in relation to the spacecraft. The solar system with the sun

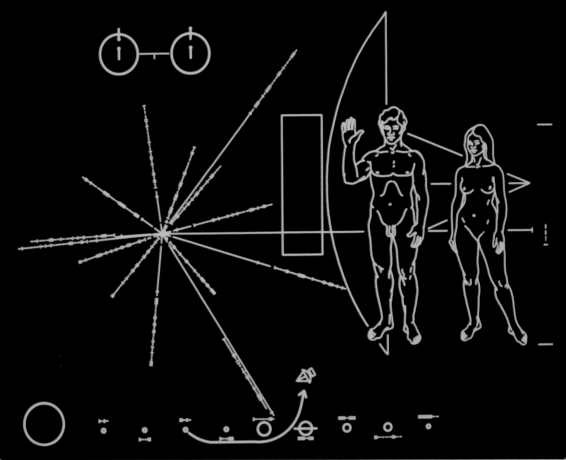

The Pioneer plaque, a pictorial message from Earth's inhabitants, journeyed into space attached to the exteriors of two Pioneer spacecraft in the 1970s. The symbol (upper left-hand corner) represents a hydrogen atom, which is the most common element in the universe. Below that, lines radiate from our sun to the relative positions of 14 pulsars. The human figures are set against the spacecraft to give scale and the man's hand is raised in greeting as a sign of goodwill.

and planets is engraved in the plaque along with a diagram showing the relative position of the sun to the center of the galaxy.

Pioneer 10 was the first manmade object to leave the solar system. NASA attached the plaque to the spacecraft's antenna support struts in a position that shielded it from erosion by stellar dust. Scientists expect the spacecraft and the plaque to survive longer than Earth and its sun. An exact replica of the Pioneer plaque was attached to *Pioneer 11* launched

The Drake Equation 50 Years Later

In 2010, on the fiftieth anniversary of first SETI project, interviewer Wilson da Silva asked Frank Drake if his famous Drake equation estimating the number of planets with intelligent life was still relevant. Drake answered:

> People keep asking, "should the equation be changed?" The answer is no. It still works. It's still correct. The only thing that's changed is the numbers we put into it. When I first invented the equation we had to guess some of the factors in the equation. A lot of those have now been established through observation. For instance the fraction of stars that have planets—we know now that it is more than half. The number of possible habitable planets in a system is higher than we thought in the past—because we've discovered things such as oceans in places we thought they couldn't exist, such as Europa.
>
> So the equation is still good. The numbers we put in it are getting more accurate all the time. There are still some big unknowns. One is the fraction of civilizations that actually develop technology.

Quoted in Wilson da Silva, "Only a Matter of Time, Says Frank Drake," *Cosmos*, April 7, 2010. www.cosmosmagazine.com.

in April 1973. After conducting flybys of Jupiter and Saturn, *Pioneer 11* traveled out of the solar system, aimed at the Taurus constellation. *Pioneer 11*'s last contact with NASA occurred in 1995 when onboard batteries ran down and became insufficient to operate the spacecraft's instruments.

An Interstellar Message

Eighteen months after *Pioneer 11*'s launch, Drake and Sagan were involved with another attempt at interstellar communications. This time the message was blasted into space from the Arecibo Observatory located high on a mountain in the jungles of Puerto Rico. The observatory hosts the world's largest radio telescope, which is operated under the auspices of the US National Astronomy and Ionosphere Center (NAIC) and the National Science Foundation (NSF). The Arecibo Observatory's 1,001-foot radio telescope (305m) is the largest ever constructed, and it is used to study the atmosphere around Earth, other planets, comets, and asteroids. The instrument is also used for SETI purposes.

The Arecibo telescope was built in 1963. After it was remodeled in November 1974 the NAIC celebrated by broadcasting what is called the Arecibo Interstellar Message into deep space. Drake and Sagan composed a message of 1,679 binary digits—that is, the ones and zeros that make up the basic language of computers. Each digit is represented by one of two radio frequencies so that it might be received like a Morse code telegraph message from the nineteenth century. The broadcast, which lasts less than three minutes, consists of seven parts. The encoded messages include the numbers 1 through 10 and the indentifying formulas of various biogenic elements, including hydrogen, carbon, nitrogen, oxygen, and phosphorus. The message also contains a simple graphic depiction of the solar system, a figure of a human, and a picture of the Arecibo radio telescope.

Because radio waves travel at the speed of light, the Arecibo Interstellar Message traveled past Mars within 1 minute of broadcast and left the solar system within 5 hours and 20 minutes. The message was aimed at the Great Cluster, which is located in the constellation Hercules about 25,000 light-years from Earth. Formally known as the globular cluster Messier 13 or M13, this densely filled region of space contains approximately 300,000 stars within a radius of 18 light-years. With such a high star density, astronomers believe M13 has a greater chance of reaching Goldilocks planets with intelligent life-forms.

Sounds of Earth

One of the most unusual CETI attempts began in 1977 when NASA launched two identical *Voyager* spacecraft weeks apart. The sister ships, *Voyager 1* and *Voyager 2*, obtained unprecedented scientific information about Jupiter and Saturn and their moons and took stunning photographs of the outer planets, including Uranus and Neptune. Nestled among the gear on both spacecraft is an identical gold-plated copper record similar to vinyl record albums popular on Earth at that time. In this era before CDs and MP3 players, each Voyager Golden Record was seen as the best way to send audio messages from Earth.

The Voyager Golden Record is titled "Sounds of Earth." It contains vocal greetings in 55 languages. Other common sounds such as the wind, the surf, a human kiss, laughter, and noises made by different animals such as crickets, elephants, and wild dogs are included. The record holds 90 minutes of music from around the world with traditional songs from Africa, the Americas, and Asia, classical music from Johannes Bach and Mozart, and even the classic rock and roll song "Johnny B. Goode," recorded in 1958 by Chuck Berry.

In addition to sounds, the Voyager Golden Record contains 116 digital images. These include various diagrams of organs in the human body, photographs of mountains and buildings, and pictures of Earth and other planets taken from space. A printed message from Jimmy Carter, who was president at the time of the *Voyager* launches, states:

> We cast this message into the cosmos. . . . Of the 200 billion stars in the Milky Way galaxy, some—perhaps many—may have inhabited planets and spacefaring civilizations. If one such civilization intercepts *Voyager* and can understand these recorded contents, here is our message: This is a present from a small, distant world, a token of our sounds, our science, our images, our music, our thoughts and our feelings. . . . This record represents our hope and our determination, and our good will in a vast and awesome universe.[38]

Cosmic Calls

The *Voyagers* passed out of the solar system in 1989 carrying the golden records that contain NASA's last official attempt at communications with extraterrestrial intelligence. Since that time, several others have sent messages into space. In 1999 Canadian astrophysicists Yvan Dutil and

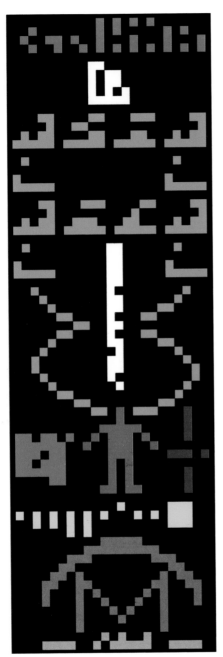

This computer-generated image (originally in black and white) was beamed into space by the Arecibo radio telescope in 1974. It contains a binary message that includes the numbers from 1 to 10 (magenta), atomic numbers for several elements (white), information about DNA (green, white, and light blue), the population of Earth (pink), a human figure (red), and the planets of the solar system (yellow).

Stephane Dumas designed a digital message, referred to as the Cosmic Call, that contained a series of symbols. The Cosmic Call described basic concepts of math, physics, chemistry, and biology. The message was sent into space from a radio telescope called the Evpatoria Planetary Radar (EPR) owned by the Russian Academy of Sciences in Evpatoria, a small town located in Crimea, Ukraine.

Several years after the Cosmic Call, another message was sent from the EPR. The Teen Age Message, or TAM, was a project organized by Russian radio astronomer Alexander L. Zaitsev in 2001. The Teen Age Message was so named because Zaitsev solicited ideas from Russian student scientists. The message was broadcast to nearby stars in three parts. The first was a low-frequency radio signal meant to help aliens detect and lock onto the transmission. The second part of the message contained seven musical selections including Russian folk songs, the 1966 hit "Good Vibrations" by the Beach Boys, and the finale of Beethoven's *Ninth Symphony.* The third part of the TAM contained digital photos and text information with greetings—in Russian and English—from the teen scientists. The message lasted 2 hours and 12 minutes and was transmitted several times between August 29 and September 4, 2001.

A Moral Goal

A second, longer Cosmic Call was sent from the EPR in 2003. Some believe such messages are futile since the Earth—and the human race—will be changed beyond recognition by the time alien civilizations could return a cosmic call. Zaitsev has formulated a reply to the skeptics: "To me, the main goal of our messaging is to bring to extraterrestrials the long-expected message that 'You are not alone!' And if everybody in the Universe would follow this moral goal, there is a hope that someday we shall get a message, too."[39]

> ### DID YOU KNOW?
>
> Over 5.2 million volunteers participate in SETI@home by running a free program that analyzes radio telescope data. This combined computing power has been acknowledged by Guinness World Records as the largest computation in history.

NASA ceased its CETI programs after the 1970s *Voyager* launches. Since that time, planetary scientists like Zaitsev have been left to carry on with the work of sending communications to extraterrestrials. However, this is not the case for SETI searches. After NASA cut all SETI programs in 1994, the search for alien signals continued with volunteers. Today many amateur astronomers are plugged into SETI@home, a computing project hosted by the Space Sciences Laboratory at the University of California at Berkeley. SETI@home allows anyone with an Internet connection to download and run a program that analyzes data produced by hundreds of radio telescopes all over the world. By consolidating the computing power of millions of machines, SETI@

home allows for a large amount of information to be processed in the homes of volunteers.

"A Lot of Life in the Universe"

On April 8, 2010, astronomers celebrated SETI's fiftieth birthday and the scientific advances that have occurred since 1960. Drake was interviewed for the occasion, and the pioneering scientist remained excited about the prospect of finding intelligent extraterrestrial life:

> The observations have all supported the idea that there is a lot of life in the universe. . . . [Almost] any civilization we find will be much older than our own. They will have much more experience. Much more knowledge, technical and scientific. And that will benefit us greatly. And we will learn ways to have a higher quality of life on earth which would otherwise take us perhaps hundreds of years of expensive research to learn, to identify ourselves.[40]

Drake estimates that at least 10,000 advanced civilizations are in the galaxy and that contact is inevitable. While no signs from "little green men" have yet been detected, the search has just begun. As SETI researchers point out, if the galaxy were an ocean, humans would have examined only about a gallon's worth of water. That leaves a massive amount of interstellar space where alien civilizations—even now—might be communicating with Earth.

CHAPTER FOUR

Extreme Environments and Extraterrestrials

In 2008 a poll by the Scripps Howard News Service revealed that 56 percent of Americans believe intelligent life exists on other planets. About 33 percent think intelligent space aliens have visited Earth, while 5 percent claim to have had a close encounter or interaction with an extraterrestrial. About three-quarters of those who have had close encounters describe the space creatures as grey aliens, or "Greys." These extraterrestrials have been featured in dozens of films and television shows including the popular 1977 movie *Close Encounters of the Third Kind.* The Greys are described as being around 4 feet tall, with greenish-gray skin, short legs, bulbous heads, and large wrap-around or slanted black eyes.

Most astrobiologists do not believe the accounts of close encounters with aliens. When they do envision extraterrestrials, most scientists likely think of single- or multicelled microorganisms related to bacteria or other earthly microbes. As science writer Joseph Hooper explains, astrobiologists are "looking for microorganisms on other planets. The search for little green men has given way to the search for little green bugs."[41]

Extreme Earthly Environments

Astrobiologists search for clues about life in the galaxy by studying some of the most extreme environments on Earth. They are looking for creatures that survive in the frigid cold, fiery heat, and the toxic chemicals similar to those found on distant planets.

Organisms that live in hostile earthly environments are called extremophiles. These microorganisms show that once life gains a foothold, no matter how precarious, it can thrive almost anywhere. Extremophiles live near volcanoes, deep beneath the oceans, on the polar ice caps, and in Earth's driest deserts. They tolerate extremely salty conditions as well as acidic and alkaline environments. Extremophiles have even been found in hazardous waste dumps and areas of high radioactivity. Some do not eat food or utilize sunlight for energy but instead survive by consuming toxic chemicals in a process called chemosynthesis.

The environmental conditions where extremophiles live are similar to those found on Mars, Jupiter, Saturn, Titan, Europa, and elsewhere in the solar system. These environments are classified in four broad categories: high and low temperatures, extreme pressure, high salt levels (salinity), and excessive pH. PH determines the acidity or alkalinity of an environment. (Lemon juice is very acidic, baking soda is somewhat alkaline, and household ammonia is very alkaline.) While complex forms of life cannot thrive in areas with extreme temperatures, pressures, salinity, or pH, microscopic life can grow in these conditions. For example, deep beneath the ice sheets of Siberia in Russia microbes called psychrophiles live in water that is colder than ice, about 23°F (-5°C). While water generally freezes at 32°F (0°C), the Siberian water remains liquid because it is extremely salty. In addition to thriving in the cold, psychrophiles survive intense pressure from living over 2 miles (3.2km) beneath the surface.

> **DID YOU KNOW?**
>
> Scientists believe that between 60 and 70 percent of all bacteria on Earth live deep within the oceans far from the sun's life-giving rays.

Astrobiologists believe that psychrophiles might resemble microbes on other planets where large ice deposits are found. According to astrobiologist Richard Hoover, "I think it is quite possible that when we go by spacecraft to collect samples from the icy moons of Jupiter or to collect

The pink color of this lake in Senegal in western Africa is a result of extremophile bacteria that thrive on very high salt levels in the water. If life can exist in extremely hot, extremely cold, and extremely salty places on Earth, scientists say, it might also exist on planets with extreme environments.

samples from the polar ice caps of Mars, we may very well find [psychrophiles]." Hoover also believes psychrophiles might have lived in the icy tails of comets "frozen there for eons until a collision with another planet or moon delivered them to a new home."[42]

Black and White Smokers

Extremophiles that live at the other end of the temperature scale are called thermophiles. These organisms flourish in extremely hot conditions found around hydrothermal vents. These vents are located around 7,000 feet (2,100m) beneath the surface in both the Pacific and Atlantic oceans. Hydrothermal vents continuously spew mineral-rich water heated to 750°F (400°C) by volcanic activity in the earth's crust. This superhot water mixes with the deep ocean water, which is only about 34°F (1°C), creating an environment where temperatures average 240°F (120°C). By comparison, water boils at 212°F (100°C), and paper catches on fire at about 450°F (232°C). While the scalding water shooting from hydrothermal vents would kill most creatures, it supports an environment teeming with microbial organisms.

Hydrothermal vents form towering structures called chimneys. These are created when the superheated minerals in the water meet the frigid undersea waters. The minerals form into particles which build up into chimneys. The hottest chimneys are called black smokers, formed by waters that are above 662°F (350°C). Black smokers are colored by iron and sulfide in the water, which combine to form an acidic black chemical called iron monosulfide. Slightly cooler chimneys, those under 626°F (330°C), are called white smokers. These chimneys are formed by the white minerals barium, calcium, and silicon. Whatever their color, chimneys can grow up to 30 feet (9m) in only 18 months and reach up to 150 feet (45.7m) in height before they collapse under their own weight.

Creatures That Thrive in Extreme Conditions

Despite the inhospitable conditions, single-cell microbes thrive in the scalding water, eating the minerals that spew from the earth's core. In the absence of sunlight, thermophiles called archaea convert the chemicals into energy through chemosynthesis.

Not all thermophiles are microscopic, and some even resemble bizarre creatures from science fiction stories. For example, hydrothermal vents host giant tube worms, which grow up to 10 feet (3.3m) in length. These creatures have no mouths and depend on chemosynthesis to survive. In this process, the tube worms absorb highly acidic hydrogen sulfide through a plume on their tails. The chemicals are processed by oozing reddish bacteria that live in the giant tube worm's digestive system. The bacteria convert the hydrogen sulfide and carbon monoxide into energy, which allows the tube worm to grow an amazing

Synthesizing Chemicals

Some extremophiles survive by a process called chemosynthesis in which they obtain energy released by chemicals to produce food. This is different than the familiar process of photosynthesis whereby plants survive by capturing solar energy in sunlight.

The most extensive ecosystems based on chemosynthesis are formed by extremophiles living in the total darkness around hydrothermal ocean vents. While deadly to most marine animals, the boiling hot, toxic, and highly acidic chemical-rich soup provides life for extremophile bacteria. These microbes absorb hydrogen sulfide streaming from the vents and turn it into sulfur. During this process chemical energy is released in the form of sugar molecules, which are consumed as food. Scientists who study chemosynthesis in extremophiles speculate that similar chemical reactions could support life in the chemical-rich atmospheres found on planets and moons.

0.08 inch (2mm) a day. Research scientist and author Clifford Pickover comments on the weird tube worms that eat chemicals in the boiling water: "It's hard to believe creatures such as these exist on Earth. In fact, when I have to design aliens for my science fiction novels, I get ideas from photographs of [giant tube worms]. There's nothing stranger on our planet."[43]

Thermophiles like the giant tube worm are of interest to astrobiologists because bodies in outer space have similar environmental conditions with extreme temperatures, acidic chemicals, and near total darkness. In theory, bacteria like those found in giant tube worms could evolve around hydrothermal vents that might be located deep beneath the water on planets with ice or liquid oceans. NASA describes how extremophile research has changed the way scientists think about life on Mars: "Martian life might not be so widespread that it would be readily found at the foot of a lander spacecraft but it may . . . [thrive] in an underground thermal spring or other hospitable environment. Or it might . . . exist in some form in niches below the currently frigid, dry, windswept surface, perhaps entombed in ice or in liquid water aquifers."[44]

Living in Acid

In addition to extreme heat, hydrothermal vents create extremely acidic environments due to the chemicals in the water. In recent years researchers have discovered unusual acid-tolerant extremophiles, or acidophiles, growing in the water of the Norris Geyser Basin, the hottest and most active geyser basin in Wyoming's Yellowstone National Park and perhaps the world. Compared to undersea hydrothermal vents, the waters of the Norris Geyser Basin are tepid, around 95°F (35°C). However, due to high levels of chemicals, the pH level of the water is acidic enough to dissolve nails.

Despite the acidic environment, scientists discovered an unusual group of microbes living inside rocks of the Norris Geyser Basin in 2005. The acidophiles belong to a family of organisms best known for causing human illnesses like tuberculosis and leprosy but do not cause disease themselves. The Yellowstone microbes are the most acid tolerant in the world and extremely rare. They get energy from the dissolved metals and hydrogen found in the hot water. Norman Pace, one of the scientists who discovered the acid-loving microbe, says, "This is another example that life can be robust in an environment most humans view as inhospitable."[45]

> **DID YOU KNOW?**
>
> The first extremophiles were observed in 1977 living in hydrothermal vents beneath the Pacific Ocean near the Galapagos Islands off South America.

Scientists believe geothermal environments similar to the one in Yellowstone may once have existed on Mars. Jeffrey Walker, another scientist associated with the Yellowstone discovery, explains the connections between the hot springs and Mars: "The prevalence of this type of microbial life in Yellowstone means that Martian rocks [found near] former hydrothermal systems may be the best hope for finding evidence of past life there."[46]

The Darkest Cave

Creatures that live in the total darkness of deep underground caves are called scotophiles. A rich example of dark-loving creatures was found in 1996 in a previously undiscovered cave in Romania. Movile Cave was closed off and separated from the rest of the world for 5.5 million years. Despite the fact that it received no energy from the sun, when researchers visited the cave for the first time they found it to be crawling with 47 different species, 30 of which were previously unknown. The creatures living in complete darkness included spiders, leeches, scorpions, and millipedes.

In addition to being completely dark, the Movile Cave ecosystem had very low oxygen levels. However, the water in the cave was rich in hydrogen sulfide, methane, and carbon monoxide. This provided a source of chemical energy for cave creatures that lacked sunshine and fresh air.

In the bizarre cave environment the scotophiles looked like aliens from another planet. Some had no eyes but grew overdeveloped antennae for sensing food, danger, and mates. Since the cave dwellers did not need to develop color for camouflage as protection from predators, some of the scotophiles were clear—their blood could be seen flowing through their bodies. Pickover believes the study of this strange environment might one day help scientists find extraterrestrials: "If we want to search for life on Mars, we must look for the Martian version of Movile Cave where liquid water could exist and light need not penetrate."[47]

> **DID YOU KNOW?**
>
> Extremophiles called halophiles tolerate very salty water allowing them to thrive in the Dead Sea in Israel, which is more than 8.5 times saltier than the ocean.

Giant tube worms inhabit a hydrothermal vent deep in the Pacific Ocean. The conditions in which these creatures live—extreme temperatures, acidic chemicals, and near total darkness—resemble conditions found on other planets.

The Driest Desert

The Atacama Desert in northern Chile is one of the harshest desert environments on Earth. With little water and blazing sunlight, the environment of the Atacama is the extreme opposite of the Movile Cave. Despite features that make the Atacama like the surface of another planet, microscopic life can be found in its burning desert sands. These bacteria-like creatures are xerophiles, the name given to extremophiles that survive in extremely dry conditions.

At 10 million to 15 million years old, the Atacama is the oldest desert on Earth and also the driest. Even the famed Sahara Desert in Africa

Extremophile Hunter Nathalie Cabrol

NASA scientist Nathalie Cabrol has climbed the 19,731-foot Lincancabur volcano (6,014m) several times. In the thin air at this altitude, most people would have difficulty performing basic tasks, such as setting up a tent. But after Cabrol reached the top of the volcano, she went diving into the frigid lake that fills the crater where she discovered extremophiles like those that might live on Mars. Cabrol set the unofficial record for the highest female dive, but setting records is not what motivates her. As Cabrol explains, she is driven to find life on other planets:

> I'm not a daredevil but I am free-diving in lakes at 20,000 feet, so you understand where I am coming from. . . . I've been around the block, the extreme block, a couple times, and I have yet to find a place where I didn't find life. Everywhere you find a hurdle, you find a way life found to get around it. . . . Thousands of generations have been wondering about life elsewhere. Were they disappointed that they didn't get a response? The answer is, they kept asking the question. What is different is that our generation might have the technological ability to find it.

Joseph Hooper, "Is This the Machine That Will Finally Find Life On Mars?" *Popular Science,* January 29, 2006. www.popsci.com.

receives about 500 times more precipitation than the Atacama, which averages less than .004 inches (0.01cm) of rain per year. Many areas of the Atacama go without rain for decades, and some places have not had rainfall for over 400 years. And unlike other deserts, the Atacama is relatively cold, with average daily temperatures ranging between 32°F (0°C) and 77°F (25°C).

Conditions in the Atacama are so dry, cold, and barren that chemical engineer Matt Ford writes, "It is the closest one can get to Mars while remaining grounded on Earth."[48] This makes the desert a perfect

NASA testing ground for robotic equipment being developed to search for life on Mars. In 2006 researchers went to the Atacama to test-drive a 6.5-foot-long, 440-pound wheeled robot (2m, 200kg) named Zo. Zo (Greek for "life") was built to detect extremophiles; it sprays special dyes on the ground that make xerophiles appear as bright patches in photos. The robot is being developed for a possible 2016 mission to Mars to search for microbial life.

The Highest Lake

One of the lead scientists on the Zo project, French-born NASA planetary geologist Nathalie Cabrol, specializes in analyzing the ancient lakebeds of Mars as possible habitats for life. Cabrol has also taken great personal risks in her search for extremophiles, climbing down into volcanoes and diving into frigid lakes.

Cabrol's focus has been a towering mountain, the Licancabur volcano, that dominates the landscape in the northern Atacama Desert. The crater at the top of the Licancabur volcano is filled with water. At 19,731 feet (6,014m) above sea level, the crater lake is the highest lake in the world. Temperatures can drop to -30°F (-34°C), and the lake remains covered with ice most of the year.

Despite the forbidding conditions, Cabrol climbed Licancabur volcano four times between 2002 and 2005. After the difficult climb, Cabrol conducted several dives without air tanks into the lake in search of extremophiles. The unnamed lake atop Licancabur has an extreme environment that combines volcanic gases, low-oxygen, high-ultraviolet (UV) radiation from the sun, and low atmospheric pressure (two times lower than at sea level). While diving under the lake ice, Cabrol discovered unique extremophiles that exist through chemosynthesis.

> **DID YOU KNOW?**
>
> Endoliths are extremophiles that live inside rocks 2 miles (3.2km) below Earth's surface. Endolith metabolisms are so slow that they only reproduce once every 100 years.

While little is understood about the Licancabur environment, it is one of the few places on Earth to study extremophiles that might exist in the ancient lakes of Mars. As Cabrol explains,

> If there was life on Mars 3.5 billion years ago, it could have used defense mechanisms similar to those used by the organisms at Licancabur volcano to survive. . . . [The volcano also] gives us clues about which planets are good candidates to search for life and help in the design of future mission strategies and technologies for exploring ancient Martian [lakes] or oceans on Europa.[49]

Higher Life-Forms

Astrobiologists believe studying extremophiles is a necessary step in the search for extraterrestrial life. Extremophile exploration techniques that lead to the discovery of living microbes elsewhere in the solar system would prove

that life can exist elsewhere. NASA's Chris McKay concludes that this life might be intelligent: "If life did start twice, independently, in our solar system [on Earth and another planet], that tells us that life starts pretty easily in the universe. If so, why shouldn't it develop intelligence somewhere else?"[50]

Astrobiologists who research the possibilities of sentient life in the universe can advance their knowledge by studying creatures on Earth. While Earth's environment might be unique, intelligent aliens would need to develop methods to communicate, feed themselves, use tools, and care for their young. And these basic survival techniques might resemble those practiced by humans or other earthly animals.

If intelligent creatures live elsewhere in the galaxy, they likely depend on familiar senses such as seeing, hearing, tasting, touching, and smelling. Aliens might also develop other senses common in fish and reptiles. These include the abilities to detect mild electrical pulses, magnetic fields, or infrared heat. As Pickover writes, "Given the diversity and range of senses on Earth, we cannot precisely predict the nature of alien senses. However, we can make educated guesses on the basis of sensory evolution on Earth."[51]

Alien Smellers

The senses developed by aliens would depend on the environment of the planet they inhabit. If extraterrestrials lived on a planet where the atmosphere was cloudy and the landscape dimly lit, they would not rely on eyesight. Instead they might perceive the world as a rattlesnake does. Rattlesnakes have forked tongues that they flick up and down to "taste" the world around them. The tongue picks up microscopic airborne particles and gases from the air that are analyzed by a gland in the snake's mouth called the Jacobson's organ. This organ can identify scents related to food, enemies, danger, or mating. Based on the way rattlesnakes evolved, it is theoretically possible that intelligent extraterrestrials might use flicking tongues to build and run their society.

Pickover believes aliens that perceive the world through a sense of smell would have very large noses. He calls these extraterrestrials Smellers. If such creatures existed, according to Pickover, they might have advantages over humans on Earth:

> Their primary sense being smell, in some ways they are better off then we are with our primary vision sense. For one thing, Smellers can know precisely how long ago you were sitting in a chair and the direction you went after leaving the chair. Olfactory communication gives information about the past and present. Once the Smellers had familiarized themselves with human structure and psychological responses, they could determine gender, health, and even moods using their sense of smell. Smellers could even use their olfactory sense to see around corners in darkness.[52]

Seeing the World

With billions of habitable planets in the universe, worlds where the sun or several suns create an environment bathed in bright light like the Atacama Desert are likely. In such an environment, intelligent aliens would theoretically develop sharp eyesight. As Lewis Dartnell writes, "Sight is an extremely important sense for perceiving one's surroundings and is thought likely to be a universal characteristic."[53] However, aliens might not see the world through what are called camera eyes, the type used by humans to view images in sharp detail. Aliens might have compound eyes like those found on insects. Compound eyes have thousands of light receptors that allow insects to perceive very fast movement. With this type of sight, an alien could see the individual beats of a hummingbird's wing or a drop of rain as it broke apart upon hitting the ground. However, if a human had compound eyes, each eye would have to be as big as his or her head in order to provide the clarity of camera eyes. This would give large aliens with compound eyes the appearance of horror movie monsters with gigantic fly eyes.

Rattlesnakes also provide an example of the way aliens might see. Rattlesnakes have special organs that perceive heat in the form of infrared rays. This allows a rattlesnake to sense the body heat given off by its prey and see a heat picture of the animal. With a highly developed infrared system, an alien would be able to see the warmth left on the ground by human footprints.

Exciting Science

Astrobiologists can formulate theories about extraterrestrial life studying snakes, flies, extremophiles, and thousands of other organisms. However, the nature of the universe remains a great unknown. Intelligent aliens might exist as beams of light or invisible smells wafting through a cloud. Whatever they may be, aliens are likely to experience the universe in an entirely different manner than humans.

While few astrobiologists expect to study a real, living extraterrestrial, the wonders of planet Earth provide exciting lessons in theoretical alien biology. As extremophile hunter John A. Baross says: "We are going after the most incredible organisms that exist. This gives us the chance to look at the most ancient, primordial events and understand how life began and to think about the possibility of extraterrestrial life. It's really exciting science."[54] Although who, or what, is out there is impossible to tell, the search for extraterrestrial life continues to be driven by the thrill of discovery on Earth.

SOURCE NOTES

Introduction: Exploring an Infinite Universe

1. Quoted in Michael J. Crowe, *The Extraterrestrial Life Debate, 1750–1900*. Cambridge: Cambridge University Press, 1986, p. 126.
2. Quoted in David Salt, "Study Predicts Trillions of Planets," Discovery, 2010. http://dsc.discovery.com.

Chapter I: Looking for Life on the Moon and Mars

3. Quoted in Crowe, *The Extraterrestrial Life Debate*, p. 210.
4. Quoted in Crowe, *The Extraterrestrial Life Debate*, p. 211.
5. Percival Lowell, *Mars*. Boston: Houghton, Mifflin, 1895, pp. 74–75.
6. John F. Kennedy, "Special Message to the Congress on Urgent National Needs," John F. Kennedy Presidential Library and Museum, 2010. www.jfklibrary.org.
7. Kevin W. Plaxco and Michael Gross, *Astrobiology*. Baltimore: Johns Hopkins University, 2006, p. 192.
8. Plaxco and Gross, *Astrobiology*, p. 193.
9. Ed Grayzeck, "Viking Mission to Mars," NASA, December 18, 2006. http://nssdc.gsfc.nasa.gov.
10. Quoted in Carl Zimmer, "Are We Alone? New Hope in the Search for Alien Life," *Popular Mechanics*, October 1, 2009. www.popularmechanics.com.
11. Quoted in Barry E. DiGregorio, "Viking Data May Hide New Evidence for Life," *Space Daily*, June 20, 2004. www.spacedaily.com.
12. NASA, "Viking 1," June 20, 2010. http://solarsystem.nasa.gov.
13. Quoted in David Hatcher Childress, *Extraordinary Archaeology*. Kempton, IL: Adventures Unlimited, 1999, p. 192.
14. Lewis Dartnell, *Life in the Universe*. Oxford: OneWorld, 2007, pp. 111–12.

15. Dartnell, *Life in the Universe*, p. 113.

16. Quoted in Ron Baalke, "Meteorite Yields Evidence of Primitive Life on Early Mars," July 2004. www2.jpl.nasa.gov.

17. Charles Schmidt, "The Chemistry of Life on Mars," ACS, 2001. http://pubs.acs.org.

Chapter 2: Space Probes, Chemicals, and Microbes

18. Quoted in Plaxco and Gross, *Astrobiology*, p. 93.

19. Quoted in Bill Steigerwald, "NASA Researchers Make First Discovery of Life's Building Block in Comet," August 17, 2009. www.nasa.gov.

20. Quoted in Steigerwald, "NASA Researchers Make First Discovery of Life's Building Block in Comet."

21. Jessica Sunshine, "Deep Impact Team Reports First Evidence of Cometary Ice," NASA, February 3, 2006. www.nasa.gov.

22. Quoted in Zimmer, "Are We Alone?"

23. Enrico Piazza, "About Saturn and Its Moons," NASA, November 12, 2010. http://saturn.jpl.nasa.gov.

24. Piazza, "About Saturn and Its Moons."

25. Dartnell, *Life in the Universe*, pp. 142–43.

26. Quoted in Cathy Weselby and Jia-Rui Cook, "What Is Consuming Hydrogen and Acetylene on Titan?" NASA, June 3, 2010. www.nasa. gov.

27. Quoted in Weselby and Cook, "What Is Consuming Hydrogen and Acetylene on Titan?"

28. Quoted in Mike Wall, "Saturn Moon's Atmosphere May Hold Ingredients for Life," Space.com, October 7, 2010. www.space.com.

29. Quoted in Zimmer, "Are We Alone?"

30. Quoted in Dennis Overbye, "New Planet May Be Able to Nurture Organisms," *New York Times*, September 29, 2010. www.nytimes.com.

Chapter 3: Scanning the Skies for Intelligent Life

31. Quoted in *Science Daily*, "Earth-Sized Planets May Be Common Throughout Our Galaxy, NASA Survey Suggests," October 29, 2010. www.sciencedaily.com.

32. Quoted in Fay Schlesinger, "Stephen Hawking: Earth Could Be at Risk of an Invasion by Aliens Living in 'Massive Ships,'" *Daily Mail*, April 10, 2010. www.dailymail.co.uk.

33. Giuseppe Cocconi and Philip Morrison, "Searching for Interstellar Communications," Cosmic Search, September 21, 2004. www.big ear.org.

34. Cocconi and Morrison, "Searching for Interstellar Communications."

35. Quoted in Wilson da Silva, "Only a Matter of Time, Says Frank Drake," *Cosmos*, April 7, 2010. www.cosmosmagazine.com.

36. Quoted in Brian McConnell, *Beyond Contact: A Guide to SETI Communicating with Alien Civilizations*. Sebastopol, CA: O'Reilly & Associates, 2001, p. 63.

37. Ronald D. Ekers et al., eds., *SETI 2020*. Mountain View, CA: SETI, 2002, p. 22.

38. Quoted in Guy Webster, "Howdy Strangers," NASA, August 19, 2002. www.jpl.nasa.gov.

39. Quoted in Morris Jones, "Astronomer Speaks Up for ET," *Space Daily*, September 29, 2002. www.spacedaily.com.

40. Quoted da Silva, "Only a Matter of Time."

Chapter 4: Extreme Environments and Extraterrestrials

41. Joseph Hooper, "Is This the Machine That Will Finally Find Life on Mars?" *Popular Science*, January 29, 2006. www.popsci.com.

42. Quoted in Kate Tobin, "Extremophile Hunter," National Science Foundation, June 1, 2009. www.nsf.gov.

43. Clifford Pickover, *The Science of Aliens*. New York: Basic Books, 1999, p. 63.

44. NASA, "Mars Exploration Rover Launches," June 2003. www.jpl.nasa.gov.

45. Quoted in Cheryl L. Dybas, "Yellowstone Discovery Bodes Well for Finding Evidence of Life on Mars," National Science Foundation, April 20, 2005. www.nsf.gov.

46. Quoted in Dybas, "Yellowstone Discovery Bodes Well for Finding Evidence of Life on Mars."

47. Pickover, *The Science of Aliens*, p. 69.

48. Matt Ford, "Chilean Extremophile Bacteria Thrive in Mars-Like Conditions," Ars Technica, March 5, 2009. http://arstechnica.com.

49. Quoted in Kathleen Burton and Diane Richards, "Licancabur, Bolivia-Chile: Exploring the Highest Lake on Earth," NASA Ames Research, October 11, 2002. www.extremeenvironment.com.

50. Quoted in "NASA Scientists Find Bacterium Can Survive on Arsenic," Environmental Protection, December 9, 2010. http://eponline.com.

51. Pickover, *The Science of Aliens*, p. 47.

52. Pickover, *The Science of Aliens*, p. 48.

53. Dartnell, *Life in the Universe*, p. 177.

54. Quoted in Nancy Touchette, "World's Hottest Microbe: Loving Life in Hell," Genome News Network, August 22, 2003. www.genome newsnetwork.org.

FOR FURTHER EXPLORATION

Books

Joseph A. Angelo Jr., *Life in the Universe*. New York: Facts On File, 2007.

David Baker, *The 50 Most Extreme Places in Our Solar System*. Cambridge, MA: Belknap Press of Harvard University Press, 2010.

Lewis Dartnell, *Astrobiology: Exploring Life in the Universe*. New York: Rosen Classroom, 2011.

J. Phil Gibson, *Natural Selection*. New York: Chelsea House, 2009.

Mike Perricone, *The Big Bang*. New York: Chelsea House, 2009.

Pamela S. Turner, *Life on Earth—and Beyond: An Astrobiologist's Quest*. Watertown, MA: Charlesbridge, 2008.

Websites

Astrobiology Institute (http://astrobiology.nasa.gov/nai). The Astrobiology Institute focuses on the study of the origins, evolution, distribution, and future of life in the universe. The website, aimed at students, features astrobiology-related current events, virtual tours, science lessons, photos, videos, and more, with contributions from over 700 researchers distributed across 150 institutions.

Astrobiology Magazine (www.astrobio.net). *Astrobiology Magazine* is a popular online science magazine published by NASA. Stories profile the latest and most exciting news across the field of astrobiology, or the study of life in the universe.

The Astrobiology Web (www.astrobiology.com). Calling itself "Your Online Guide to the Living Universe," this site contains the latest breaking news in the search for extraterrestrial life. Updates and archives provide information about recent discoveries along with photographs and other fascinating astrobiology info about Earth, comets, and distant planets.

NASA (www.nasa.gov). The website of the world's premier space exploration organization contains extensive information about past and current missions to the moon, the outer planets, planetary moons, and comets. Readers can learn about the high-tech equipment used by NASA and view updated photos and information from the latest rendezvous with distant objects in the solar system.

SETI@Home (http://setiathome.ssl.berkeley.edu). This site is home to enthusiasts who wish to volunteer their unused computer power for analyzing data collected by radio telescopes throughout the world. By combining millions of computers into a single project, researchers hope to hear extraterrestrial communications accidentally picked up by telescopes engaged in other research.

SETI Institute (www.seti.org). The mission of the SETI Institute is to explore, understand, and explain the origin, nature, and prevalence of life in the universe. The site has information on astrobiology, interstellar communications, and features podcast radio shows about cutting-edge space exploration and communications.

INDEX

Note: Boldface page numbers indicate illustrations.

PICTURE CREDITS

ABOUT THE AUTHOR

Stuart A. Kallen is the author of more than 250 nonfiction books for children and young adults. He has written on topics ranging from the theory of relativity to the history of rock and roll. In addition, Kallen has written award-winning children's videos and television scripts.